Amigos de la granja / Farmyard Friends

LOS POLLOS
CHICKENS

Maddie Gibbs

Traducido por Eida de la Vega

PowerKiDS press

New York

Published in 2015 by The Rosen Publishing Group, Inc.
29 East 21st Street, New York, NY 10010

First Edition

Editor: Caitie McAneney
Book Design: Katelyn Heinle
Spanish Translator: Eida de la Vega

Photo Credits: Cover, p. 1 Jon Beard/Shutterstock.com; p. 5 Jordan Tan/Shutterstock.com; pp. 6, 24 (rooster) PCHT/Shutterstock.com; p. 9 Nataliia Melnychuk/Shutterstock.com; p. 10 BestPhotoPlus/Shutterstock.com; p. 13 John Panella/Shutterstock.com; p. 14 Kemeo/Shutterstock.com; p. 17 wavebreakmedia/Shutterstock.com; p. 18 Amy Kerkemeyer/Shutterstock.com; p. 21 cynoclub/Shutterstock.com; p. 22 holbox/Shutterstock.com; p. 24 (vegetables) Symbiot/Shutterstock.com.

Library of Congress Cataloging-in-Publication Data

Gibbs, Maddie, author.
Chickens = Los pollos / Maddie Gibbs.
pages cm. — (Farmyard friends = Amigos de la granja)
Parallel title: Amigos de la granja.
In English and Spanish.
Includes index.
ISBN 978-1-4994-0273-5 (library binding)
1. Chickens—Juvenile literature. 2. Domestic animals—Juvenile literature. I. Title.
SF487.5.G55 2015
636.5—dc23

Manufactured in the United States of America

CPSIA Compliance Information: Batch #CW15PK: For Further Information contact Rosen Publishing, New York, New York at 1-800-237-9932

CONTENIDO

CONTENTS

Muchas granjas tienen pollos. ¡En todo el mundo, los pollos se crían como alimento!

Many farms have chickens. Chickens are raised for food all over the world!

cresta
comb
barbillas
wattle

Los gallos son los pollos machos. Los gallos tienen una **cresta** en la cabeza. Tienen **barbillas** debajo del pico.

Roosters are male chickens. Roosters have a **comb** on their head. They have a **wattle** on their chin.

Un pollo hembra se llama gallina. Una gallina pone cerca de 300 huevos al año.

A female chicken is called a hen. A hen lays about 300 eggs every year.

Los pollos pequeños se llaman pollitos. Salen de los huevos.

Baby chickens are called chicks. They break out of eggs.

La mayoría de los pollos de granja vive en corrales llamados gallineros.

Most farm chickens live in pens called coops.

Los granjeros alimentan los pollos con semillas, **verduras** y granos, ¡pero también les gustan los insectos y los gusanos!

Farmers feed chickens seeds, **vegetables**, and grain. They love bugs and worms, too!

Los granjeros crían pollos para tener huevos y carne. ¡También son buenas mascotas!

Farmers raise chickens for their eggs and meat. They also make great pets!

Los pollos Plymouth Rock tienen plumas rayadas. Son originarios de América.

Plymouth Rock chickens have striped feathers. They first came from America.

Los pollos sedosos tienen un pelaje espeso y suave. ¡También son juguetones y divertidos!

Silkie chickens are very fluffy. They're also friendly and fun to watch!

Los pollos no solo viven en granjas. ¡Los puedes tener en el patio de tu casa!

Chickens don't just live on farms. You can keep them in your backyard!

PALABRAS QUE DEBES SABER
WORDS TO KNOW

(la) cresta
comb

(las) verduras
vegetables

(las) barbillas
wattle

ÍNDICE / INDEX

SITIOS DE INTERNET / WEBSITES

Due to the changing nature of Internet links, PowerKids Press has developed an online list of websites related to the subject of this book. This site is updated regularly. Please use this link to access the list: www.powerkidslinks.com/fmyd/chic